LET'S WA
Series Edito

Wales

Lawrence Garner

Line drawings by
Kathy Gittins

JAVELIN BOOKS
POOLE · NEW YORK · SYDNEY

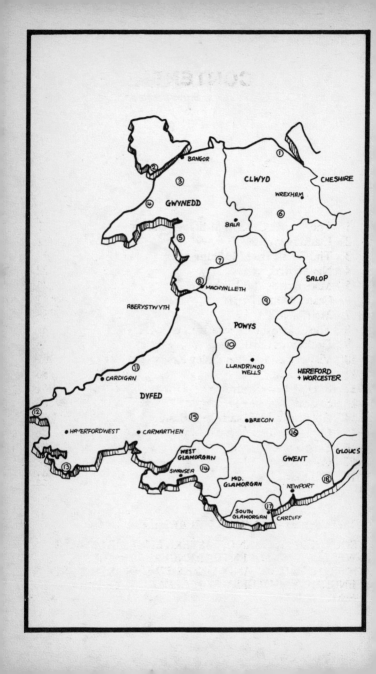

DISTRICT

①
BANGOR
②
③
④
GWYNEDD
⑤
⑦
⑧
MACHYNLLETH
ABERYSTWYTH

CLWYD
WREXHAM
⑥
BALA

CHESHIRE

SALOP

⑨

POWYS

⑩
LLANDRINOD
WELLS

HEREFORD
+ WORCESTER

⑪
• CARDIGAN
DYFED

⑫

⑮

• BRECON

⑯

• HAVERFORDWEST   • CARMARTHEN

GLOUCS

⑬

WEST
GLAMORGAN
⑭
SWANSEA
MID.
GLAMORGAN

GWENT
NEWPORT •
⑱

⑰
SOUTH
GLAMORGAN
• CARDIFF

CONTENTS

The complete **LET'S WALK THERE** Series

SOUTHERN ENGLAND; EASTERN ENGLAND; SOUTH
WEST ENGLAND; CENTRAL ENGLAND; WALES;
NORTHERN ENGLAND; YORKSHIRE & NORTH WEST
ENGLAND; SOUTHERN SCOTLAND; NORTHERN
SCOTLAND

First published in the UK 1987 by Javelin Books,
Link House, West Street, Poole, Dorset, BH15 1LL

Copyright © 1987 Javelin Books

Distributed in Australia by
Capricorn Link (Australia) Pty Ltd,
PO Box 665, Lane Cove, NSW 2066

British Library Cataloguing in Publication Data

Garner, Lawrence
  Wales —(Let's walk there)
  1. Wales —Description and travel—1981-
  — Guide-books
  I. Title   II. Series
  914.29'04858   DA735

ISBN 0 7137 1774 2

Cartography by Ron Rigby

Cover picture:
Nant Gwynant courtesy of The British Tourist
Authority, Britain on View (BTA/ETB)

Typeset by Inforum Ltd, Portsmouth
Printed in Great Britain by Cox & Wyman Ltd, Reading, Berks.

INTRODUCTION

As worthwhile as any walk might be, it becomes doubly appealing if it takes you to some place of special interest. The nine books in this series, covering England, Scotland and Wales were conceived to describe just such walks.

A full description of the walk's objective is given at the start of each chapter. The objectives are diverse, giving a wide choice. Most are non-seasonal, and involve little walking in themselves once you are there.

Following the description of the objective, each section of the walk is clearly described, and a specially drawn map makes route-finding straightforward. As well as detailing the route, the authors describe many subsidiary points of interest encountered along the way.

The walks are varied and easy to follow. None of them is too taxing, except in the severest weather. Most are circular, returning you to your car at the starting point. Family walkers with young children will find plenty of shorter routes to suit their particular needs, whilst those with longer legs can select from more substantial walks.

The routes have been carefully chosen to include only well-established routes, and readers will certainly increase the enjoyment which they and others derive from the countryside if they respect it by following the Country Code.

Bruce Bedford
Series Editor

Walk 1
THE GRANGE CAVERNS
MILITARY MUSEUM
HOLYWELL, CLWYD
5 miles

A military museum may not be everyone's idea of an interesting day out, but the Grange Caverns Military Museum is
definitely different. For a start it is underground – in an old
mine where remarkable skill on the part of the original
miners has left a marvellous array of pillars and arches
reminiscent of a cathedral crypt.

Once there, you realise that the seventy or so war-scarred
vehicles within would be quite out of place in a bright well-
polished building and are seen to much better advantage in
these rough-and-ready surroundings. The dramatically-lit
interior also makes possible other features, such as the
reconstruction of a World War 1 trench or a garden air-raid
shelter. The vehicles dominate the museum, but an inner
room contains thousands of smaller items such as weapons,
uniforms, badges, medals and touching personal documents
and mementos. It is all very professionally done, right down
to the music of Vera Lynn and Glenn Miller in the NAAFI
Canteen – a very comfortable cafe.

The museum is open every day from Easter to October and
at weekends during February and March. Remember – the
temperature underground is always cool, so woollies are
necessary.

The walk to the museum is part rural, part urban and part
suburban and encounters a ruined abbey, an industrial
heritage park, a spectacular view and a religious shrine.

As you drive into Holywell centre take the B5121 (sign-

GRANGE CAVERNS MILITARY MUSEUM

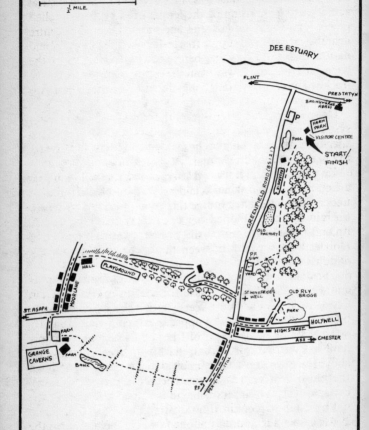

½ MILE.

DEE ESTUARY

FLINT

PRESTATYN

BASINGWERKS ABBEY

P

FARM PARK

POOL

VISITOR CENTRE

START/ FINISH

GREENFIELD ROAD (B5121)

STABLES

OLD FACTORY

P.F. SIGN

YARD

ST. WINIFRIDES WELL

OLD RLY BRIDGE

HALL

PLAYGROUND

MOOR LANE

ST. ASAPH

FARM

PARK

HIGH STREET

HOLYWELL

A55 CHESTER

GRANGE CAVERNS

FARM

BANK

P.F.

FELIN-Y-BALL TRAIL

N

-----	ROUTE
═══	ROAD
↦─┤	STILE
▨	SLOPE
⋈	BRIDGE

posted Greenfields) and leave the car in the Heritage Park car park towards the bottom. You are at the northern end of a long narrow valley that was an early centre of industrial activity. A stream running the length of the valley supplied power for a variety of factories and mills. The visitor centre near the car park will supply free leaflets on the industrial and natural history of the valley before you begin walking on the wide path that leads away from the centre. This was once the trackbed of a railway, and though the rise is gentle enough for the walker it seems impossibly steep for a train.

On the right are the remains of the valley's elaborate water system, with various pools, reservoirs and sluices interspersed with what is left of the factory buildings. Otherwise, the path seems entirely rural.

Keep to the main track and after about half a mile you pass a fine section of original retaining wall on the left and go under a double-arched bridge that used to carry a road over the railway track. On the other side take the path that curves up and back to the top of the bridge. Turn left and enter Holywell High Street between the Midland Bank and Ye Olde Boar's Head.

Turn right, cross the High Street, and walk down to its end, where Cross Street forks left. Take the first on the left in Cross Street (Pen-y-Ball Street) which brings you up to the busy A55. Almost directly opposite is Pen-y-Ball Hill.

This is the steepest part of the walk, although you only have to cope with a short stretch of it. This high ground above the town saw much mining and quarrying, and among the plush new houses on the Hill are some old workers' cottages, and it is also possible to see some remnants of the old roadside walls built from quarry waste.

After about 250 yards a public footpath sign points to the right. Pass through a gate here and receive your reward for the climb – a sensational view of the Dee estuary with the Irish Sea beyond. The Wirral peninsula stands out clearly on the far side, but its low hills mask the city of Liverpool behind it. The vast sand dunes show vividly why the Mersey superseded the Dee as a major trading river.

World War 2 vehicles displayed underground at the Grange Caverns Museum

The hillside path now runs along a low earth bank with a spasmodic hedge through rough pasture (there are grassed-over spoil tips just below). At the next hedge cross the official-looking stile mysteriously marked 'Private Water' and then pass through two more small fields with similar stiles. The fourth field is much larger and the path is barely perceptible; you should continue on the same line across the middle, making for an earth bank on the other side. There is an inconspicuous stile tucked away here. Follow the earth bank along the top of the next field and descend gently towards a farm. The path avoids the farm buildings on the left and passes in front of a small white cottage. A final stile brings you into the car park of the museum.

After your visit the route is down the museum's entrance drive, across the A55 and down Moor Lane opposite. At the bottom of this road a footpath leads off to the right just beyond a small community hall and runs beside a children's playground. After 200 yards a wide track begins on the left; ignore this and continue on the narrow path through a belt of bushes. This area also shows signs of the old workings that lie beneath the modern outskirts of Holywell. Very soon the path joins a wide gravelled lane which in turn acquires tarmac and leads into Greenfield Road.

You emerge opposite Holywell's oldest attraction, St Winifride's Well. It gave the town its name and has been a place of pilgrimage for centuries. For a modest sum you can enter the shrine and see the well, where the water of legendary curative powers rises.

To complete the walk go down Greenfield Road for 50 yards and through a yard indicated by a public footpath sign. The path on the other side joins the old railway track on which you started. The day can be concluded with a stroll down to the extensive ruins of the twelfth-century Basing-werke Abbey. Alternatively the little farm park next to the visitor centre will compensate children who may have had to put up with dad's army reminiscences.

LLANDDWYN ISLAND
ANGLESEY, GWYNEDD
5 or 2¾ miles

Although the interior landscape of Anglesey is unspec-
tacular, its coastline is of great interest, in particular the vast
area of sand at its southern tip, known as Newborough
Warren.

In the days when nature was in control here up to 100,000
rabbits a year were caught in these shifting dunes, but in
recent years the planting of conifers and marram grass has
stabilised the whole area, and it is now a 1,500-acre nature
reserve. To the west of the Warren is a romantic peninsula
connected to the mainland at high tide by a thread of rock.
This is Llanddwyn Island, an exhilarating place to be at most
times of the year.

The island first became famous as the sanctuary of the
fifteenth-century St Dwynwen, traditionally a patron saint of
lovers, whose shrine was a popular object of pilgrimage.
More recently it housed a pilot station and lighthouse. Both
elements of its history have left relics that can be explored
today, including a ruined church, the lighthouse, the lifeboat
station and a row of pilots' cottages. Nature provides added
attractions such as stark rocks and sandy coves.

Access to the area for vehicles is strictly limited. From the
village of Newborough a single lane leads through a forest to a
large parking area behind the dunes. From here on all
exploration must be on foot, and there are two possible ways
of walking to the island. The shorter route is directly along
the shore (for once the description 'miles of sandy beach' is

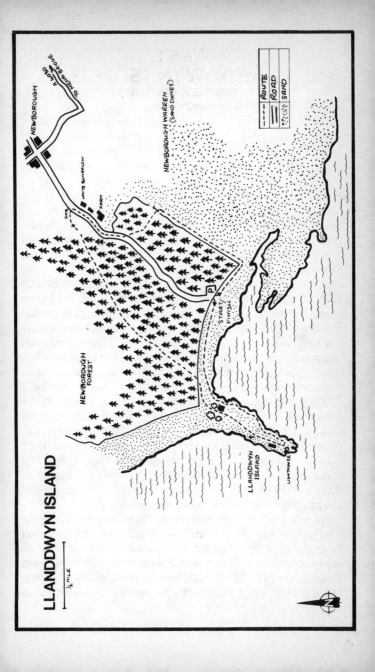

LLANDDWYN ISLAND

½ MILE

ROUTE	ROAD	SAND

NEWBOROUGH

TO MENAI BRIDGE

A LODG

WHITE BUNGALOW

FARM

GATE

NEWBOROUGH WARREN (SAND DUNES)

NEWBOROUGH FOREST

P

START

FINISH

LLANDDWYN ISLAND

LIGHTHOUSE

accurate) but the longer walk described here gives you an opportunity to look at the work that has gone into taming this wilderness.

Walk from the parking area to the beach, turn left and reach the south-eastern corner of the forest. A track leads away from the sea to follow the forest boundary while the peculiar lunar landscape of the dunes stretches away on the right. The random humps, now covered by marram grass, show vividly the effect of high winds on loose sand over centuries. The thickly-planted conifers are, of course, another effective stabiliser.

After about three-quarters of a mile look out for a stile in the forest fence. It gives access to a 'ride' that cuts into the plantation and brings you out on the road to the car park. Turn right and follow the road for about half a mile past a farm and then a prominent white bungalow on the right. Just after this a steel gate to the left opens onto an area of heathland. (There is no signpost, but two caravans in a garden mark the right gate.) From here a discernible track curves back towards the forest edge, which you enter by way of a waymarked stile next to a wide gate.

The path you are now on runs for nearly two miles to the sea. It is wide and open and passes through a surprisingly varied range of trees in different stages of maturity. Half-way along it becomes a broad track ending in the inevitable sand dunes, from which you emerge onto the beach with Llanddwyn Island slightly to your right. The entrance to the island is guarded by rock outcrops, worn by the sea over millions of years but still remarkably convoluted; they are reminders that Llanddwyn is composed of Pre-Cambrian rock, the oldest in Britain.

The landmark to make for is a small hut beyond the rocks. The broad path runs past it, and as you come over the first rise a tall cross is silhouetted dramatically against the skyline, with the lighthouse visible in the background. Down on the right the jagged rocks show the danger to any small craft hugging the coast. The cross stands opposite the ruins of a small church built in rubble construction and with one

*The old lighthouse overlooks one of the many
inlets on Llanddwyn Island*

window surviving. It was built in the sixteenth century to
replace an earlier church dedicated to St Dwynwen, and the
Victorian cross presumably commemorates the people who
once worshipped here. Today, Soay sheep graze around the
church.

The approach to the headland is marked by a row of tiny
cottages, built in 1810 for the Llanddwyn pilots and later
used by lighthouse keepers. In one of them the Nature
Conservancy Council has installed a small visitor centre
explaining the history and natural significance of the island,
while another has been imaginatively furnished in Victorian
style by members of local Women's Institutes. The cottages
are fascinating places, with their tiny staircases leading to
bedrooms that are little more than shelves. The cannon
standing outside was formerly used to summon the lifeboat
crew.

Unfortunately it is not possible to enter the disused light-house, which in its later days was automatic, but you can climb up to its base and peer inside at the spiral staircase disappearing upwards. This is also a good place to enjoy the views of the rocky headland spread out below and the distant mountains of Snowdonia. The second cross visible behind the lighthouse is also Victorian and commemorates St Dwynwen. A square stone building – the old lifeboat station – stands above a small cove reminiscent in summer of a Cornish fishing village as the sailing craft bob at their moorings.

Llanddwyn is a most enjoyable place with plenty to explore. When the time comes to return you can take a path that branches right at the cottages and follows the indented shore on the eastern side. It is an up-and-down progress requiring more energy than the main path, but it takes you past secluded coves frequented by sea birds.

The parking area is reached by walking along the sands.

Walk 3
THE WELSH SLATE MUSEUM
LLANBERIS, GWYNEDD
5½ miles

The North Wales slate industry may have declined, but its history continues to fascinate visitors. Some of the sites now open to the public are extravagantly presented, but not so the Welsh Slate Museum at Llanberis. As a branch of the National Museum of Wales its authenticity is guaranteed, and its displays are sober and factual. It is situated on a vast plateau at the western end of the great Dinorwic quarries at the junction of Padarn and Peris, the two lakes of Llanberis. At one time 3,000 men worked here, and the quarries continued production until 1969. Consequently it was possible to preserve a good deal of equipment and keep many of the installations intact.

The museum is housed in Victorian buildings that are unusually sophisticated in style, and the exhibits display all the processes of slate production. But the museum itself is only one attraction on a site that is now part of the Padarn country park. The narrow-gauge railway that runs the length of the lake has its terminus here. The steep Vivian quarry with its many galleries rises above everything else, and the quarry hospital, perched on the hillside to the west, can also be visited. Even out of season this is a fascinating place.

The walk to the site involves a complete circuit of Llyn Padarn, and the ideal starting point is at the extreme western end of the lake. Drive out of Llanberis on the Caernarfon road and take the first turning on the right after two miles. Turn right again immediately and you are on a closed-off

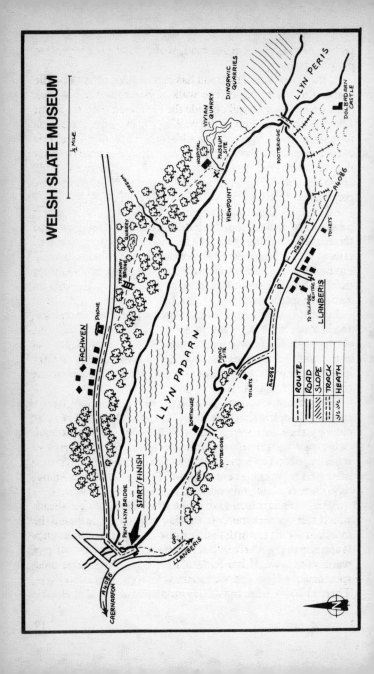

section of the former main road, which makes a convenient parking place.

At the point where the road has been fenced off a step-stile marks the beginning of the walk. Once round a big rock outcrop you have to walk beside the new main road for about 100 yards before a gap in the wall on the left provides access to steps leading down to the trackbed of the former Llanberis branch line, ideal for walking. It is interesting here to study the old quarrying community of Fachwen on the hillside opposite, with its random scattering of dwellings fringed by tiny walled fields.

After following the trackbed for a quarter of a mile you pass a large, silent and forbidding pool on the right and then an iron footbridge over the path – obviously a relic of railway days. It appears to give access to a boathouse and not much more, but as you walk a little further you discover that a bulging promontory here has been converted into an elaborate picnic site.

You can walk through the site, but you have to join the new access road eventually, and it is here that you get your first glimpse of the objective – the Dinorwic quarries at the far end of the lake. Immediately ahead, Dolbadarn Castle stands on its low mound and the first houses of Llanberis appear on the right.

The walk now rejoins the main road for 100 yards before entering a large lakeside car park. At the far end of it take the path by the water's edge and pass through a little park. A swing gate on the other side leads to an extensive area of water-meadow, and the footpath passes through three iron gates (at the first one note the remains of a slate fence – long, thin slabs of slate embedded upright in the ground).

After the third iron gate make for the footbridge ahead, which marks the entrance to the Padarn country park and the museum site. It is worth pausing on the bridge to look round. It appears to cross a river, but in fact this is the narrow strip of water connecting Llyn Padarn with Llyn Peris. The most spectacular part of the old quarry workings faces Llyn Peris. There is little on the outside to indicate that a hydro-electric

19

Slate-splitting, demonstrated at the Welsh Slate Museum

power station is buried within the mountain. It is a pumped storage scheme involving Llyn Peris and another lake above the quarries; at peak periods of demand water is released from the top lake to drive the turbines, and when demand is slight the water is pumped up again for re-use.

If you wish to visit the ruins of Dolbadarn Castle now is the time, because it is within easy walking distance. Dolbardan is a native Welsh castle of the thirteenth century, unusual in an area where the castles were more often built by English invaders.

Cross the bridge and pass into the museum area. As the Victorian buildings come into view the first impression is of quality: the first building on the left has elaborate iron glazing bars, while the museum itself is almost distinguished in its architecture.

Start the return walk by climbing the approach road to the quarry hospital (it starts beside the railway station, and the platform half-way up is one of the best viewpoints on the lake). At the building turn left across its front and make for the squat stone hut – the mortuary – in the corner of the garden. From here a path leads into trees, rising at first and then beginning a long descent to a cascading stream. Cross the primitive bridge and follow the main track up past an abandoned farm and through a steel gate.

A small quarry lies behind the vegetation on the right. An old tramway bridge crosses the path, then the track turns sharp right and rises to join a minor road in the village of Fachwen. Turn left and walk through the village, with its splendid views, including Snowdon away to the east.

Most of the cottages in Fachwen have been modernised, some out of all recognition, but a few retain their original lumpy and primitive appearance and hint at the realities of hovel life. Once through the village the pleasant lane descends uneventfully and returns you to the starting point by way of the old four-arched Pen-llyn bridge.

Walk 4
NANT GWRTHEYRN
LLEYN PENINSULA, GWYNEDD
2½ miles

As you drive from Caernarfon into the Lleyn Peninsula, perhaps on the way to Pwllheli, you notice a three-peaked mountain looming ever closer. This is Yr Eifel, and it marks the beginning of an area that has traditionally been regarded by local residents as 'separate', with its own peculiar atmosphere – a sort of brooding remoteness. It may be this atmosphere that makes visitors seek the south coast of Lleyn rather than the north. Certainly you can walk on the northern shores for a long time without seeing another human being.

There is one small valley in particular that always seems haunted. Nant Gwrtheyrn runs down to the sea at the foot of Yr Eifel, and you approach it by turning off the A499 Caernarfon-Pwllheli road at Llanaelhaearn, continuing for three miles to Llithfaen on the B4417 and then turning right up a minor road for one mile to a Forestry Commission car park. A notice forbids motor vehicles to go any further.

Legend has it that the fifth-century British king Vortigern came here to die after being deposed. That may be so, but the more obvious reason for the melancholy air of the valley is the fact that within living memory it was a thriving community. A tiny, self-contained village called Porth-y-nant was built on the sea shore to accommodate the workers who extracted the granite-like stone from the hills above. A pier provided a rudimentary harbour from which the stone could be transported (the road was far too steep) and complex inclines linked the workings with the beach.

NANT GWRTHEYRN

½ MILE

PORTH-Y-NANT

'GREEN'

DERELICT FARM

CHAPEL

TO BEACH

TRAMWAY

BEACH

QUARRY

*NO CARS BEYOND
THIS POINT

P

START/FINISH

INCLINE

B4417

LLITHFAEN

→ TO
A499
(2½m)

- - - -	ROUTE
———	ROAD
\\\\\	SLOPE
=====	TRACK
	HEATH

N

When the quarries closed this almost inaccessible hamlet died with them. An idealistic scheme to make Porth-y-nant a centre for the study and promotion of the Welsh language has led to the restoration of the chapel and one or two cottages, but the two terraces, at right angles to each other and facing on to a small 'village green', are still mainly derelict. The attraction of the walk to Porth-y-nant lies partly in nostalgia, partly in a long stretch of sandy beach and partly in a wealth of industrial relics, fascinating to anyone remotely interested in this aspect of history.

From the car park follow the metalled road that curves down to the left through a gate. The road is fairly new and was built to give a less severe gradient; you can see the original track branching off to the right soon after the gate.

The first hairpin bend opens up an impressive view of a cliff-like rock wall with a stream falling almost vertically. On the valley floor a derelict farm with a complicated pattern of walls catches the eye, and towards the sea the village is already visible. At the next bend the other end of the old track emerges steeply, and you begin to appreciate the sheer difficulty of getting out of the valley in the old days.

After the second bend it is a short walk past the abandoned farm to the village. On the outskirts ruined buildings are half-concealed by undergrowth, but the chapel and the large house on the other side of the road look deceptively normal. It is only as you pass between them that the open roofs and boarded windows of the terraces become obvious. At the far end is a much grander detached house, built possibly for the quarry manager. One of the terraces slopes down to the sea, and although the cottages are vertical the communal roof follows the slope – no doubt saving a good deal of money, but giving the terrace an odd crooked look.

From here you can either make your way down to the beach or walk south from the chapel along a tramway track cut into the hillside. The rails are still in place, and the trucks that ran on them are scattered haphazardly in the quarry they served. Winding gear still stands above the tramway and derelict buildings on the shore indicate the final destination

Yr Eifel, the mountain range that looms behind Nant Gwyrtheyrn

of the stone. Further along the track is an elaborate walled incline and chute, with more trucks heaped about as though on the last working day the men had simply released them down the incline as a final gesture before starting the last walk home. It is possible to wander among these workings for a long time while the beach-lovers enjoy themselves in their own way.

Theoretically there is an alternative return route, discovered by scrambling up beside the other quarries to the north of the village and walking round the top of the valley, but it is not recommended for any but the most fit and active. Most visitors will be content to stroll back the way they came, still perhaps haunted a little by this strange place.

Walk 5
MAES ARTRO CRAFT VILLAGE
LLANBEDR, GWYNEDD
4½ miles

On the west coast of Wales, to the south of Harlech, there is a network of runways called, rather grandly, the Royal Aeronautical Establishment. At one time it was RAF Llanbedr, and lines of long barracks, offices and mess-halls stood just outside the village.

By the 1970s the disused buildings were decaying quickly, but a project was formed to use the site as a centre for craftsmen, and restoration began just in time. The result is a place that will entertain both adults and children. Craft workshops cover pottery, leatherwork, weaving, knitting and jewellery, while elsewhere are a model village in an ingenious grotto, a sea-life aquarium, a vintage amusement arcade, a pets' corner, a group of re-created traditional Welsh shops and a collection of sturdy wooden structures for children to clamber on. It is all pleasantly haphazard, but there is nothing amateurish about the refreshment arrangements, which are very good indeed.

A single admission fee gives access to everything, but before Easter and after September it is worth phoning to check that the village is open. (Out of season it functions on a limited scale, but you may get in for nothing.)

The walk to Maes Artro begins at Llandanwg, on the shore about two miles south of Harlech. You reach it by turning off the A496 at Llanfair; this minor road ends in a car park just behind the beach.

Start the walk by returning a little way along the road to a

MAES ARTRO CRAFT VILLAGE

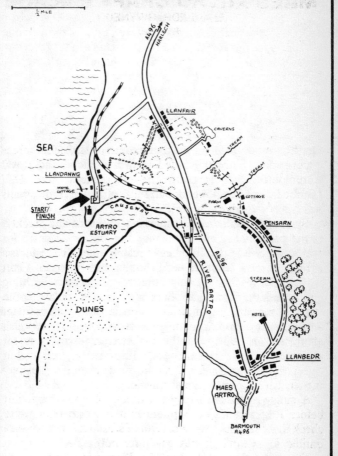

½ MILE

SEA

HARLECH
A496

LLANFAIR

CAVERNS

STREAM

STREAM

LLANDANWG

WHITE COTTAGE

START/FINISH

CAUSEWAY

ARTRO ESTUARY

FARM

COTTAGE

PENSARN

A496

RIVER ARTRO

STREAM

HOTEL

DUNES

LLANBEDR

MAES ARTRO

BARMOUTH
A496

N

‐ ‐ ‐ ‐	ROUTE
══════	ROAD
⊢━⊣	GATE
⊢ ‐ ‐ ⊣	STILE
⅊⅊⅊	HEATH
∞∞∞∞	ROCKS
▪▪▪▪	RAILWAY

low white cottage on the left. Immediately opposite is a stile with a public footpath sign. The path beyond soon crosses the railway line – in operation, so caution is necessary. Two more stiles in quick succession bring you into a field which you cross diagonally, aiming at a gap in the wall in the far corner. Once through this you find yourself in a very pleasant green lane lined by dry stone walls, evidently an old right of way for cattle or sheep.

As the lane climbs gently towards Llanfair the view ahead is dominated by old quarries above the village, although Llanfair itself has been considerably smartened up. The lane reaches the village street beside a chapel. Turn right along the main road, passing a garage on the right and a phone-box on the left. About 100 yards later watch out for a footpath leading off to the left (the public footpath sign is there but invisible from this direction) and follow it as it climbs easily towards the quarries. It reaches the bottom of the workings, turns sharply right and continues to join the zig-zag road that is the main quarry entrance.

A diversion is possible here because some of the underground caverns in the hillside above are open to the public and can be reached by going up the entrance road. Otherwise, cross the road and walk along a wide artificial plateau, past quarry buildings that have apparently been converted for agricultural use. You are now on another old workmen's path, this time leading to the hamlet of Pensarn. The track crosses a narrow stream, passes along the top of a scree-covered slope and emerges into a field, running level on a contour. The age of this right of way is shown by the old iron kissing gate which you come to next.

Once through it you may not find the path easy to detect, but it runs straight ahead, over another stream by way of a pile of stones, past a farm on the right and up a gentle slope to a cottage. Don't be deterred by the prospect of walking through the cottage's front garden; the gates on each side are clearly designed for public use. A concrete drive and gravelled lane now lead down into Pensarn, another old community transformed by modernisation.

Spinning, one of the many crafts featured at Maes Artro

Turn left at the junction with the minor road, pass through the village and take the right fork where the houses end. This is a pleasant, unfrequented lane that runs between stone walls along the bottom of a plantation of mixed woodland. The land on the right is low-lying rich pasture, and beyond it the dunes stretch away to the sea. On the outskirts of Llanbedr turn right at the road junction and walk the few yards to the village centre.

Llanbedr is a stolid place, full of square Victorian stone houses and largely given over to the holiday trade. Turn left on reaching the A496. Almost immediately you come to Llanbedr's most striking feature – the fast-flowing river Artro, noisy and impressively wide as it passes under the road bridge into its estuary. The next turning on the right after the bridge is the entrance to Maes Artro, marked by a squat building.

Unfortunately it is not possible to walk back to Llandanwg

by way of the sea shore, so the first part of the return route has to be back along the lane to Pensarn, unless you want to brave the traffic on the A496. This time ignore the path by which you entered Pensarn and continue on the lane until you reach its junction with the main road. Turn left and immediately right down a lane that crosses the railway. Ahead of you is the entrance to an adventure centre and sailing school. Walk in, pass round the back of the buildings to the right and through a wide steel gate.

This brings you out into a field beside the estuary, which is really an attractive small harbour dotted with sailing craft. You get a better view having crossed the field and climbed onto the causeway that confines the river at high tide. Follow the causeway to its end near the car park.

Incidentally, you will have noticed a little church right on the dunes next to the car park. It is the medieval parish church of Llandanwg, still occasionally used but half-buried under blown sand for much of the year.

Walk 6
CASTELL DINAS BRAN
LLANGOLLEN, CLWYD
4½ miles, or shorter alternative

The ruins of Castell Dinas Bran lie on the summit of a conical hill at 1,000 feet above sea level overlooking the town of Llangollen. Such a superb defensive site could hardly be disregarded, and a fort existed here in the Iron Age and possibly even before. The early Normans built their own structure within the boundaries of those remains, but the present remains date from the late thirteenth century.

Little evidence has been found of warlike action at Dinas Bran and it seems to have declined quickly in importance – in 1540 the traveller John Leland found it 'all in ruins' – but its remote and romantic situation inspired a good deal of legend. A local bard's tribute to the beautiful Myfanwy Vechan, who lived there at the end of the fourteenth century, has become one of the best-known of early Welsh poems. The castle's romantic appeal is still strong. It is the atmosphere and splendid setting rather than the sparse and undramatic ruins that inspire hundreds of people each year to climb the 750 feet from Llangollen.

You start in the town, and it is best to park in the big central car park off the main street near the traffic lights. Walk down to the famous Dee Bridge (thought to date from 1345 but much altered over the years) where the white water foams and swirls menacingly. As you cross note the railway station to the left on the north side of the river; it has been restored as the headquarters of a preservation society which runs steam trains over a short length of line.

31

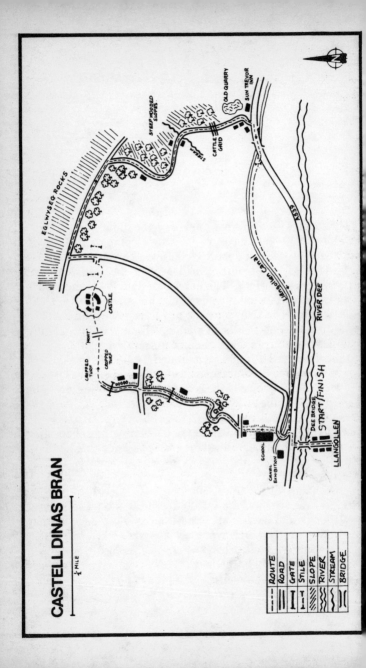

CASTELL DINAS BRAN

¼ MILE

EGLWYSEG ROCKS

STEEP WOODED SLOPES

OLD QUARRY

SUN TREVOR INN

CATTLE GRID

WHEELS

CASTLE

'MOAT'

CROPPED TURF

CROPPED TURF

SCHOOL

CANAL EXHIBITION

LLANGOLLEN

DEE BRIDGE

START/FINISH

Llangollen Canal

A 539

RIVER DEE

| ROUTE |
| ROAD |
| GATE |
| STILE |
| SLOPE |
| RIVER |
| STREAM |
| BRIDGE |

Once over the bridge turn right, cross the road and walk up Wharf Lane. As you pass over the canal the start of the path to Dinas Bran (signposted as a public footpath) is directly in front of you. The path is narrow with a tarmac surface at this stage and runs beside the extensive buildings of a secondary school. As you approach a minor road with two cottages the objective of the walk appears high up to the right, looking discouragingly distant, though this is rather illusory. Cross over the road and continue up the snaking path that now loses its tarmac and levels out somewhat as it skirts the pasture on the left. At this point a splendid view of the famous Horseshoe Pass opens up ahead, particularly striking when silhouetted againt a late evening sky.

After passing an isolated cottage you reach a gate across the path, and it is worth pausing here to look back over Llangollen, surrounded by impressive hills. The path now runs between hedges and into trees before reaching a second minor road. Continue straight across and up a stony track with a wall on the right until you reach the gate marking the end of the track. You now move out on to open hillside, on a level plateau carpeted with velvety cropped turf.

The castle is directly above, looking suddenly very close, but what catches the eye more dramatically is the immense length of limestone cliffs to the north. They are the Eglwyseg Rocks, much higher than Dinas Bran and looking almost artificially constructed with their stepped layers of stone revealed on the face. The broad sweep of green hills to the south marks the line of the Dee valley.

It takes a certain amount of resolve to leave this idyllic spot and face the final climb to the castle, especially as you have first to go down into a deep trench like a moat, but this stretch is not quite as severe as it looks from a distance. The natural steps created by generations of walkers are a great help.

The castle was obviously small, limited by the narrow confines of the summit, and the remains are skeletal. There are sections of perimeter wall, a length of interior wall and the suggestion of gates and arches, but the ruins are less

Dinas Bran castle on its romantic hilltop site above Llangollen

important than the fact that this is one of the finest view-points in Wales. To the west the mountain ridges recede towards Snowdonia, to the north the Eglwyseg Rocks loom massively, while to the east the view is up the Dee valley and well into Shropshire.

The descent from the castle is on the eastern side, directly opposite the path by which you came up. Go straight down and make for the prominent stile, after which the path is through scattered woodland and on to another stile giving access to a metalled lane. If you wish to curtail the walk, this lane, to the right, is the shortest way back to the starting point; otherwise, turn left and walk the 100 yards to a T-junction. Turn right and follow the level lane running under the limestone cliffs (what looked like a smooth expanse can now be seen to be very rough, with some huge boulders perched in a slightly alarming manner).

Continue until the lane divides and take the right fork – the start of a long and gradual descent to the valley floor. After a quarter of a mile two houses stand at a sharp right turn where a stream falls noisily and passes under the road. From this point you become aware that you are walking on a terrace with steep cliffs to the left and a sharp drop on the right. This was a quarry area and you pass several old cottages converted with varying degrees of ruthlessness.

A cattle grid marks the last stage of the lane. Just past a disused quarry on the left a sudden hairpin bend brings you to the junction with the A539. More importantly, perhaps, it brings you to the Sun Trevor Inn, which has tables on a terrace and is an excellent place for family refreshments.

Turn right at the main road and walk the short distance along the pavement to a canal bridge. A stile here allows you on to the towpath and provides a tranquil stroll back to the starting point of the walk. The canal was built by Thomas Telford in the early 1800s as a feeder channel for the canal system to the east, which is why there is an unusually constant flow of water. The water is taken from the Dee at the Horseshoe Falls – a weir to the west of Llangollen. For those interested in the subject there is a canal exhibition in Llangollen, a few yards from the Wharf Lane Bridge.

Walk 7
MEIRION MILL
DINAS MAWDDWY, GWYNEDD
3½ miles

Dinas Mawddwy is an old quarry village tucked away among high mountains about nine miles east of Dolgellau. When the slate industry declined an attempt was made to substitute cloth manufacture here, and the present Meirion Mill survives from that project. The mill now operates on a small scale and visitors may see the weaving process and purchase the products in a showroom on the premises.

Set in dramatic scenery on the site of a terminus of one of those shaky but stubborn branch railways that were once such a feature of Wales, the site provides a pleasant and interesting focus for a walk that is modest in length but of great scenic variety.

Meirion Mill lies beside the A470 on the southern outskirts of Dinas Mawddwy. You enter through the remnants of an impressive gateway, and reminders of railway days catch the eye at once. Just inside the gate is the passenger platform, and the tarmac below it has not entirely concealed the traces of sleepers below it. The station buildings have been restored as a snug coffee shop. A goods shed, complete with canopy, stands in the middle of the yard. The line was originally built in the 1860s to carry slate six miles down the Dyfi valley to the main line at Cemmaes Road, and after an early demise it recovered to run until the the 1950s.

The mill is in a restored stone building, and there is free admission to an observation platform where visitors can watch the machines at work. The shop is vast, with a very

MEIRION MILL

½ MILES

FOEL BENDDIN

LAKE VYRNWY

PICNIC SITE

OUTCROP

FARM

START FINISH

P.F. SIGN

VIEWPOINT

OLD QUARRY COTTAGES

DINAS MAWDDWY

RIVER DYFI

RUIN

FORESTRY TRACK

CEMETERY

SCHOOL

| ROUTE |
| ROAD |
| GATE |
| SLOPE |
| RIVER |
| BRIDGE |
| TRACK |

BUCKLEY PINES HOTEL

YHA

MEIRION MILL

OLD PACKHORSE BRIDGE

CARAVAN SITE

A.70

MACHYNLLETH

DOLGELLAU

A.70

N

wide range of desirable products. The interest is mainly feminine, though there is a small corner where men can buy tweed hats.

In addition to a dog exercise path and a children's play area there is another attraction here that should not be missed. Opposite the cafe at the gate a flight of steps leads down to the river to provide a view of the superb two-arched packhorse bridge built in 1635.

The circular walk starts at the point where the road leading west out of Dinas Mawddwy joins the A470. The car can be left in a layby here, and a public footpath sign stands at the bottom of some steps disappearing into the plantation above. The first 100 yards of the path are fairly steep, but this is just about the only real exertion you will be called upon to make. When the track emerges onto a broad forestry road there is a magnificent view up the valley of the River Cerist, which joins the Dyfi just below. Immediately opposite is the massive bulk of Foel Benddin, while the valley itself is bounded by steep-sided hills with tumbling streams.

The route is now to your left downhill along a terrace cut out of a hill that looms almost vertically above you. The trees on the left soon thin out to provide a view to the east of rounded green hills backed by the bare ridge of Mynydd Copog. The valley floor becomes visible, too, with the Dyfi curving through it. There are sheep everywhere, and the view sums up the hill farm economy, showing the bleak, unfenced tracts of high grazing, the lower pastures laboriously improved over the years, and the lush riverside grassland used for hay or silage. In human terms the most significant features below you are the stark cemetery, with its slate gravestones, and the school.

The forestry track descends gently to the main road. The junction is a busy little centre in itself, with a garage, a Youth Hostel and the elegant Buckley Pines Hotel opposite. Turn right and walk the few yards down the main road to Meirion Mill on the right-hand side.

After your visit cross the river bridge and enter the lane immediately on the left. It runs through a small caravan site

Meirion Mill, on the site of the former Dinas Mawddwy railway station

but is a right of way. If you turn and look back towards the mill the only signs of the intensive slate quarrying are occasional patches of scree among the conifers – man and nature have effectively obliterated the reason for the existence of Dinas Mawddwy.

The lane continues through a steel gate. This is a most enjoyable stretch of easy walking beside the tree-lined river, with healthy-looking hill pasture on the other side. The almost-perfect dome of Foel Benddin dominates the view ahead, and there are receding peaks and ridges on all sides. After a quarter of a mile the lane runs through a natural plantation of richly varied trees, at the end of which comes the best view of Dinas Mawddwy. It consists of a single long street lined with houses and cottages in various styles but built, with few exceptions, in the local grey stone. Three large chapels stand out prominently.

The lane now snakes gently upwards until a sharp left turn

marks the approach to a farm. Down on the left a ruined cottage shows evidence of an unusually high standard of stonework, while just beyond it a white house bears huge cryptic initials and the date 1838. At the point where the lane becomes the farm entrance the footpath goes straight ahead through a steel gate, passes a big rock outcrop and curves to the left as a sunken track between high hedges. This short stretch ends at the river bank, but a kissing gate gives access to a narrow path that brings you to a modern footbridge. This is a good opportunity to admire the river Dyfi, still in its infancy here with beautifully clear water chattering over the shallow, stony bed.

On the other side of the bridge is an informal picnic site which you pass through to reach the road that climbs the few yards to the village. You pass the northern end of the village street, where one corner is occupied by tiny quarrymen's cottages, converted inside but retaining their rugged exterior. Walk the short distance up to the A470 to reach the starting point.

Walk 8
THE CENTRE FOR ALTERNATIVE TECHNOLOGY
MACHYNLLETH, POWYS
4½ miles

Forget its forbidding name – the Centre for Alternative Technology is one of the most interesting and enjoyable places in Wales for a family visit.

It was founded in a derelict quarry at a time when self-sufficiency was all the rage and people were preoccupied with problems such as energy conservation and pollution. These may no longer be obsessions but the problems remain, and the centre is dedicated to the philosophy that life can be much cleaner, healthier and cheaper than we choose to make it.

It is a place that will appeal to anyone who has ever fantasised about the 'good life' or, more prosaically, has ever suffered from our reliance on centralised fuel supplies that can be cut off at any time. It will be enjoyed by those who are the slightest bit mechanically-minded, who are interested in gardening or small-scale agriculture, or who simply want to make the house warmer.

On its compact reclaimed site the centre has a wide variety of exhibits. Wind generators and solar panels feature prominently, and the conservation house is particularly interesting, with its massive insulation, quadruple glazing and other developments that result in minimal heating costs. Older power sources such as water and steam are revived. The organic vegetable gardens are a revelation, being established on unpromising soil and fed with a variety of natural fertilisers and composts that produce flourishing growth.

41

CENTRE FOR ALTERNATIVE TECHNOLOGY

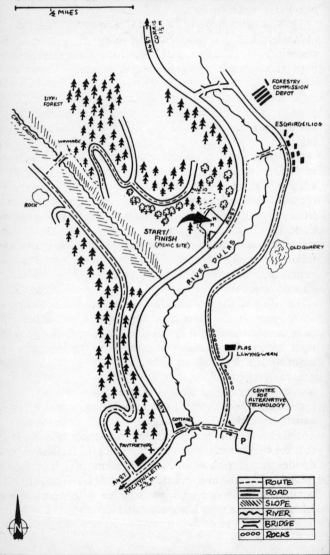

½ MILES

A487 CORRIS 1½ m

DYFI FOREST

CWM CADIAN

WAYMARK

ROCK

No 10

START/ FINISH (PICNIC SITE)

A487

RIVER DULAS

FORESTRY COMMISSION DEPOT

ESGAIRGEILIOG

OLD QUARRY

PLAS LLWYNGWERN

CENTRE FOR ALTERNATIVE TECHNOLOGY

P

A487

COTTAGE

PANTPERTHOG

A487

MACHYNLLETH 2¼ m

- - - -	ROUTE
═══════	ROAD
/////	SLOPE
～～～	RIVER
═══	BRIDGE
oooo	ROCKS

N

Elsewhere there is a smallholding with attractive buildings and appropriate poultry and animals, and a demonstration of woodland management.

The centre is situated off the A487, about three miles north of Machynlleth. It stands above the valley of the River Dulas opposite part of the vast Dyfi Forest, and the walk described here takes in a part of the forest that is open to the public.

Park at the Forestry Commission picnic site beside the A487 about three and a half miles north of Machynlleth (you need to watch carefully for the signpost). There are usually leaflets here that will make the first part of the walk more informative.

The path starts unromantically behind the public conveniences and climbs away to the right, rising gently in a series of zig-zags. At this stage it is very enclosed and passes through mixed woodland abounding in moss and tree stumps from previous plantings. If you ignore tempting diversions that look like short cuts you will soon emerge onto a wider track at forest trail marker number 10. Turn left here and follow the track. It continues to wind slowly upwards and brings you to a hard-surfaced road designed for heavy forestry vehicles.

Turn left again, go round the corner, to a sudden sense of open space as the road runs down a plateau with a fine panorama of distant hill ranges, the Dovey valley over to the right and the Dulas valley at your feet. The trees close in again at a hairpin bend, and about 300 yards after it watch for a rutted track branching away from the road on the right. It is not waymarked, but after a quarter of a mile you see a reassuring yellow arrow directing you onto a narrow path, which descends to a footbridge.

This bridge, idyllically situated in a shady glen, is probably the only direct route across the valley (Cwm Cadian) that divides this stretch of hillside. Traditionally the valley is thought to be part of the route taken by St Cadfan in the fifth century on his way from Tywyn to his outlying church at Llangadfan, many miles to the east.

The footpath now leads up to a junction with a firm track.

*One of the 'windmill' generators at the Centre for
Alternative Technology*

Turn left here and walk past a huge rock outcrop to the point
where the track joins a hard-surfaced road and starts to
descend. (The road branching to the right leads to a house, a
reminder that here and there in the forest people still live in
isolated settlements that date from long before the systematic
planting of trees.) There now follows a straightforward
descent with increasingly close views of the Dulas valley until
a final hairpin bend brings you to the A487 in the tiny hamlet
of Pantperthog.

A short distance up the road to the left is the signposted
lane to the centre. It drops down to a bridge over the Dulas,
passing an interesting example of a primitive (and probably
self-built) cottage, and ends in the car park of the centre.

After your visit turn right at the end of the Centre entrance
drive and start walking up the quiet lane on the east side
of the river. In these rather wild surroundings it is a sur-

prise to pass the aristocratic box hedges that screen Plas Llwyngwern. Note too the variety of building styles evident in the wall that makes up the frontage – many different hands have done their best to get an elegant result with the slate waste from the quarries. Down on the left there is a good view of the river as it tumbles over weirs and natural rapids.

The lane skirts a fine plantation of mixed woodland before dipping sharply to pass through old quarry workings, a pleasant spot with the river running close by. As you climb out of the dip the village of Esgairgeiliog can be seen ahead. It was obviously once a quarry settlement, but is today dominated by the big Forestry Commission depot. The houses huddle together round the usual quota of chapels and the pub. After passing the pub look out for the signpost indicating a path to the left that crosses the river on a foot-bridge and comes out on the A487.

From here it is a short walk down the road to the starting point, but note as you go two widely-differing examples of technology – the giant CAT wind generator up on the hill to the left and the surviving stretches of old slate fence that still line the road in places.

Walk 9
DOLFORWYN CASTLE
NEWTOWN, POWYS
4 miles

Dolforwyn is probably the least-visited castle in Wales. Perched on a hill overlooking the Severn valley to the north-east of Newtown, it is screened by trees and difficult to reach by car, so until recently it had been left to moulder quietly. Not that there is a great deal to see – some humpy earthworks, low walls and a few standing fragments – but it is of some interest in being genuinely Welsh. It was built in 1273 by Llewellyn ap Gruffydd, Prince of Wales, and was captured by the Normans shortly after. It seems likely to have been built as an observation post because it commands superb views up and down the Severn valley, one of the great strategic corridors into Wales.

So why visit it? Well, for a start there is that view, but there is also a sense of satisfaction in having tracked down an historical site that is virtually unknown, especially when the walk to it encounters another ambitious project that, for the moment at least, is equally secretive. This is the Montgomeryshire Canal, built in the early nineteenth century to link Newtown with the Ellesmere Canal in Shropshire.

The starting-point for the walk is at Abermule, four miles north-east of Newtown on the A483. Abermule is in fact bypassed, but beside the A483, where the northern access road to the village branches off, there is a layby for parking.

A few yards up this access road a stile takes you onto the canal towpath, and it is worth stopping at once to inspect the

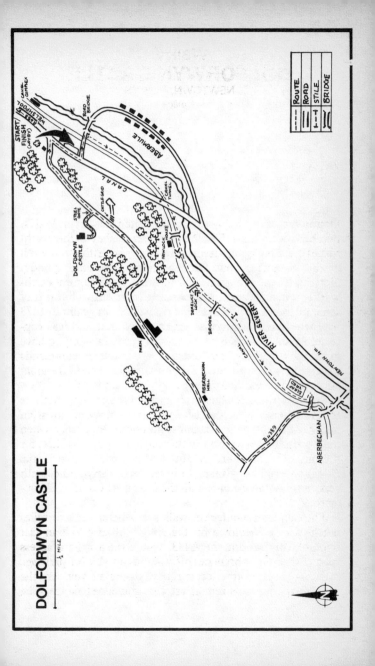

DOLFORWYN CASTLE

½ MILE

‑ ‑ ‑	ROUTE
═══	ROAD
⊢⊣	STILE
⌒	BRIDGE

START/FINISH (CP 89)

MELTSHOE

CANAL COMPLEX

ROAD BRIDGE

ABERMULE

ABERMULE

CANAL

CANAL TUNNEL

CATTLE GRID

STEEL GATE

DOLFORWYN CASTLE

NEWLOCK GATE

RIVER SEVERN

TRAPELOCK LOCK

BRIDGE

CANAL

FARM

ABERBECHAN HILL

OLD RLY YARD

B 4389

NEWTOWN 4 m.

ABERBECHAN

N

iron-ribbed road bridge over the adjacent River Severn. Vegetation covers the date, but the span has a vast inscription proclaiming it to be the second iron bridge built in Montgomeryshire.

As you move off southwards along the towpath you are very conscious of the river next to you, shallow and chattering over stones in a manner very different from its majestic progress further downstream. You are likely to be even more conscious of the road just above you and may even hear a train pass close by, because at this point the road, canal, river and railway all run within a few yards of each other, emphasising the Severn valley's importance for communications.

After 200 yards the towpath meets the road. The canal continues in a short tunnel designed to accommodate a narrow boat, but the walker has to cross the road and rejoin the path on the other side. The tunnel was a reluctant concession when the new road was built; no official seriously thought that boats would ever pass this way again after 50 years of disuse, but at the time of writing there is a scheme to reopen the whole canal.

On the other side, with the towpath gradually leaving the road, the steep forested hill on one side and low-lying meadows on the other produce an idyllic landscape. At New House lock the mechanism seems in good condition and the lock-keeper's cottage is occupied – a pleasant situation enhanced by the river, which has moved in close again after a brief meander.

You now enter a stretch that few people ever see. Trees crowd the right bank and overhang the canal, and peace descends, disturbed only by families of ducks or the bleating of sheep. The next bridge is built sturdily of stone, but it leads nowhere in particular and the lock behind it is derelict. The following bridge is more cheaply built of wood and was intended for the benefit of the landowner whose property had been divided by the canal. Now, to follow the contour, the canal is cut out of the hill and banked on the lower side.

After a stile, the stretch beyond is something of a wilder-

The well-hidden ruins of
Dolforwyn Castle

ness with straggling vegetation threatening to engulf the canal. The first sign of approaching 'civilisation' is the unexpected sight of a tractor buried in the hedge – then one or two more, and finally a whole scrapyard where tractors obviously come to die. This is the canal settlement of Aberbechan.

A low bridge enables you to cross the canal, and after a few yards the lane beyond joins the B4389. Turn right and walk up the hill. After 500 yards a minor road branches off to the right and begins a gentle climb that slowly opens up the view. Behind you is countryside typical of the Welsh border – small, hummocky hills with wooded tops overlooking hidden valleys – while to the right a wide expanse of the Severn valley comes into sight.

The lane passes Aberbechan Hall, with its odd Victorian Tudor appearance, and continues to wind gently upwards until it reaches a large farm. This is the highest point of the walk, and a half-timbered labourer's cottage looks out over a panorama of the valley. The attention is equally likely to be caught by the magnificent plantation of deciduous trees straight ahead, a stunning sight in Autumn.

An abrupt dip takes the lane into a deep dingle from which it rises to skirt the plantation, and after a quarter of a mile look out for a long cattle-gridded drive leading to a house up on the right; very shortly after it on the left is an unmarked tubular-steel gate that is the way to the castle. Now follows the final climb up a rough track that emerges on to a broad hilltop and leads round to the castle, hidden to the end.

After your visit continue down the lane, passing further examples of the fine timber plantations that have been a feature of the walk. Just before rejoining the A483 notice the black and white cottage, fancily decorated in a fashion characteristic of the border country. Before turning right on the A483 back to the starting point, it is worth walking the short distance to the left to see the little canal complex of bridges, locks, warehouses and cottages that have been well restored.

Walk 10
VISITOR CENTRE, ELAN VALLEY RESERVOIRS
POWYS
4¼ miles

The phenomenal growth of Birmingham in the second half of the nineteenth century led to many social problems, including an inadequate local supply of clean water. Birmingham Corporation devised a bold and ambitious solution – to pump water from a series of vast reservoirs in one of the high-rainfall areas of Wales.

It was not the first such project. Liverpool Corporation had already flooded a valley further north to create Lake Vyrnwy, but the Birmingham plan was more complex, involving a chain of five lakes in the Elan and Claerwen valleys. The land was bought, the few inhabitants were rehoused in a new village, and work began in 1893. In 1904 Edward VII officially inaugurated the scheme, although it was not until 1907 that the first four reservoirs began to operate. The fifth, the Claerwen, was connected in 1952.

Leaving aside the political and social implications there is no doubt that the scheme has produced a magnificent landscape feature covering thousands of acres. The Elan valley has a wild, unspoilt beauty and the artificial works are unobtrusive, being mainly in weathered stone that blends easily with these rocky uplands. The statistics are awesome; an average of 2,000 million gallons are impounded, and over 75 million gallons a day are pumped to Birmingham, still leaving enough to maintain the River Elan at its required level. A good deal of work also goes into conservation and agriculture on the land around the reservoirs.

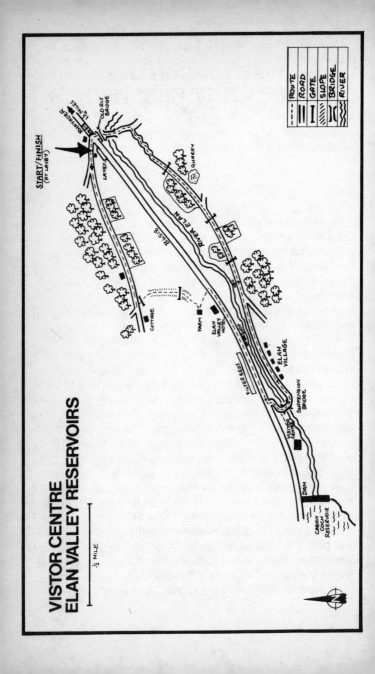

Obviously a car is needed to tour the whole area in a reasonable time, but the focal point of the system is near Elan village, lying beneath the Caban Coch dam. It is a tranquil place in the summer, but very different after heavy winter rain when the whole face of the dam foams with white water. A good visitor centre has been set up here to explain the history and working of the reservoirs, and this helps to make Elan an ideal objective for a walk.

Drive to Rhayader, which lies seven miles north-west of Llandrindod Wells, and at the town centre crossroads take the B4518 signposted to Elan Valley. One and a half miles out of town there is a crossroads marked by a raised layby on the right with a postbox. You can park here (but leave room for the postman to get his van past).

Start walking up the lane that leaves the main road next to the layby. It passes one or two houses then curves round to begin an easy rise along the northern side of the valley. This is a very attractive stretch with extensive views of the valley on the left, highlighting the contrast between the rough hillside and the lush pasture of the broad valley floor. Very soon the lane enters plantations of deciduous trees, running between mossy banks, and a break in the trees on the left brings a glimpse of mountain ranges far up the Claerwen valley.

The plantations end at an isolated cottage, and for the first time you get a clear view of the hilltop on the right. It looks very close – a surprising indication of the height you have climbed without noticing. The straggling copse that now lies above you has not been a success; it is exposed to the full force of the weather and its growth has been stunted, the trees twisted and bent by the prevailing wind.

At the point where a lane branches to the right pass through the gate opposite. It leads on to a field track that drops sharply, becoming a sunken lane between hedgebanks – a sure sign that it is an old drovers' route, no doubt used in the past for driving sheep between the upper and lower pastures. Pass through a gate and follow the lane to a farm, where it doubles back to meet the B4518.

A short stretch of walking along this road is now unavoid-

The Caban Coch dam
overlooks the Elan Valley visitor centre

able, but it is pleasant enough and there is plenty of room at
the side. Note the old railway embankment below the road.
The track was installed to ferry men and materials during the
construction of the dams. Soon after the Elan Valley Hotel
you pass a large house and a chapel, and then a sign indicates
the valley's only shop. The massive wall up on the right
contains the filter beds that are the first in a series of
purifying processes between here and Birmingham. Turn off
left here and pass the suspension bridge to reach the visitor
centre.

Begin the return walk by crossing the elegant bridge over
the River Elan and passing through Elan village. The Corporation took some pains in rehousing the inhabitants of the
flooded valley, creating a model village. At the far end is a
village green, where the lane climbs briefly through stunted
trees to join a level road signposted to Rhayader.

This traffic-free road is ideal for walking, running level on a contour with a steep wooded slope to the right and a generous view across the valley on the left. Soon after you join it note the contrast between the rough and improved pastures below; a rare dry stone wall among the hedges has been made from cleared stones of all shapes and sizes.

After two gates ignore the fork to the right. The lane now starts a gentle descent, passing a small disused quarry. Just as the mountain view over your shoulder disappears another opens up ahead across the lower valley to the distant uplands beyond Rhayader, but in the immediate vicinity the neat green fields indicate that you have reached the valley floor. The lane now starts a series of sharp bends, the last of which brings you to a river bridge and a well-preserved arch that carried the old railway line. Walk beneath it to the main road and your starting point.

Walk 11
LLANGRANOG
DYFED

4 miles

The coastline of Cardigan Bay is not as dramatic as the Pembrokeshire coast further south, but it is rather more hospitable, and its many inlets have encouraged the development of small harbours and shore settlements. The more accessible of these – Aberaeron and New Quay for example – have become celebrated resorts in the Cornish style, losing much of their fishing port atmosphere. Llangranog, seven miles south-west of New Quay, is still unspoilt, perhaps because its parking capacity is too limited to make commercialisation worthwhile.

It lies beneath one of the finest headlands on this stretch of coast. The Lochtyn peninsula is National Trust property and is surmounted by the ancient encampment of Pendinaslochdyn, which overlooks the jutting promontory of Ynys Lochtyn. Llangranog itself is no longer a harbour, but its inviting sandy beach is firmly enclosed by protective cliffs on each side. A straggle of old cottages lines the shore, and behind them other unpretentious dwellings rise haphazardly to form a village of great charm and character. There is a pub and a restaurant, but none of the usual seaside paraphernalia – it is just a place to walk, swim or simply idle the time away in tranquil surroundings.

The walk to Llangranog starts at the National Trust car park that serves Penbryn beach, a short distance to the south-west. The simplest way to reach it is to turn off the A487 onto the Tresaith road at a point about seven and a half

LLANGRANOG

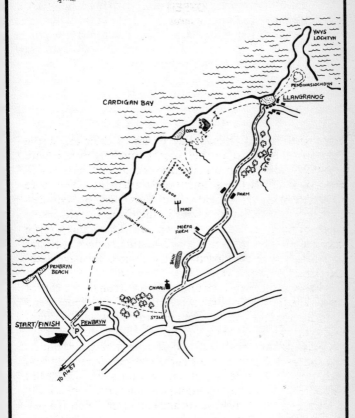

YNYS LOCHTYN

PENDINASLOCHDYN

LLANGRANOG

CARDIGAN BAY

COVE

MAST

FARM

MORFA FARM

BANK

CHAPEL

PENBRYN BEACH

STILE

START/FINISH   PENBRYN

TO A487

½ MILE

N

-----	ROUTE
=====	ROAD
⊢--⊣	STILE
∷∷∷	SAND
~~	STREAM

miles north-west of Cardigan. At the first T-junction turn
right and follow the signs to Penbryn. In the summer months
you will need to arrive early to be sure of a parking space.

Leave by the beach exit, but immediately outside the car
park gate turn right onto a waymarked field track that rises
towards the cliffs. After 200 yards the path forks; continue
straight ahead (signposted to Penmorfa Chapel) and a few
yards later pass through a red gate into a lane that skirts a
farmhouse. The lane has a distinctive turf-capped wall on the
left made up of stones set herringbone fashion into the earth –
a method designed to allow vegetation to extend its roots
downwards and bind the wall together.

Where the wall ends take the green lane branching to the
left. It runs along a plateau cut out of a steep hillside, with
woodland above and a slope to a tiny valley below. After
dropping briefly to the level of the stream this pleasant path
rises again to a narrow gate and winds its way through a thin
belt of bushes before arriving at a minor road. Cross the stile
here and turn left.

A chapel now comes into view, a surprisingly grand building for such an out-of-the-way spot. Even grander are some
of the elaborate memorials in the graveyard, presumably the
work of a local craftsman of unusual talent. At the road
junction after the chapel turn left and continue the gentle
climb that eases you gradually out of the valley. Note here the
earth bank running across the field on the left like a miniature
Offa's Dyke, a striking survival of an ancient enclosure. The
view that now opens up is of the attractive pastoral countryside that lies behind the coast. Not so long ago it would have
been given over entirely to sheep, but there are signs now of
cereal cultivation. Half a mile later the lane runs through a
sprawling farm.

After this there is a distinct change of landscape as the lane
reaches the top of a wooded ravine and begins a sharp descent
down one side. The tiny stream at the bottom seems out of
proportion to the magnificent valley, planted with fine trees
on one side and covered with bracken and gorse on the other.
A turn brings a sudden glimpse of Llangranog and the sea,

*The secluded beach at the old port
of Llangranog*

and you arrive there a few minutes later through a series of
hairpins. As you enter the village you will see a vintage
railway carriage converted into a bungalow.

If you wish to explore the Lochtyn peninsula before
turning back, a well-trodden path starts on the beach and
passes behind the seafront restaurant – quite a steep climb
but offering exceptional views to those who persist.

The return to Penbryn starts on the road by which you
arrived, but at the second hairpin take the signposted path
onto the cliffs. Care will be needed with young children on
the first stretch, which is unfenced and close to the cliff edge,
but the path soon moves inland to a safer distance. After the
first stile there is a long, low bank ahead of you; follow it
down the hill and round its bottom end into a shallow gully.
At the foot of this follow the hedge round to the left to reach a
second stile. On the other side strategically placed steps help

you down the steep slope into a deep valley. This is in fact a tiny, secluded cove with its own postage-stamp beach, accessible only on foot and a delightful place for a rest.

To get up the other side take the path that moves inland, traversing the slope. At the top of the hill it doubles back to meet the corner of a stone wall. Pass round this and make for the next corner. The path now disappears, but you pick it up again by walking slightly uphill across the field, well away from the radio mast on the left, to reach a third stile. The final stile is now visible ahead, and having crossed it you start a steady downward walk with widening views of Penbryn beach until you meet the farm track leading back to the car park.

Walk 12
ST DAVID'S CATHEDRAL
DYFED
6 miles

St David's Cathedral has a special place in Welsh history. The country's patron saint is reputed to have been born in this remote south-western tip of the country and to have founded the monastic establishment that was the forerunner of the cathedral. Although vulnerable to attacks from Norsemen it became renowned as a centre of learning and was important enough to warrant a visit from William the Conqueror in 1081. As a result it was incorporated into the Province of Canterbury as a regular cathedral foundation, the headquarters of a vast diocese that covered much of south Wales, and was a notable place of pilgrimage in the middle ages.

The visitor today will get little sense of this former greatness. The 'city' of St David's is little more than a well-developed village, and the cathedral sits unobtrusively in a hollow at its western edge, its size at odds with the small community above and behind it. Welsh Black cattle graze almost up to its walls, and the view beyond is across bare fields to the sea. But the sleepy, idyllic setting is misleading – the cathedral remains a vital diocesan centre as well as being the parish church of St David's.

Space does not allow a detailed description here of the cathedral and its associated buildings, but literature is available inside and at the City Hall. It is enough to say that there is no more rewarding place to visit in south-west Wales, and the walker can re-create something of the excitement and

ST DAVID'S CATHEDRAL

½ MILE

ST. DAVID'S HEAD

CARNLLIDI

WHITESANDS BAY

P

B4583

START/ FINISH

PEMBROKESHIRE COAST PATH

FARM

B4583

MANSION

ST. DAVID'S

BUNGALOW

TRELEDDYN

BISHOP'S PALACE

CROSS SQUARE

CATHEDRAL

TO ST. JUSTINIANS

FARM

GOAT STREET

GLANRLAN

GATE COTTAGE

RIVER ALUN

PORTH CLAIS

- - - -	ROUTE
———	ROAD
∿∿∿	RIVER
∞∞∞	ROCKS

N

anticipation that the early pilgrims must have felt as they approached one of the great sacred places of the western world.

An attractive starting-point for the walk is Whitesands Bay, the popular bathing and surfing beach to the north-west of St David's. There is a large car park reached by way of the B4583, although you need to get there early at the height of the holiday season.

Start by walking back down the road, passing a pair of incongruous suburban semi-detached houses, survivors of the pre-planning days. Keep straight on at the road junction at the top of the hill. The landscape now visible on all sides is typical of the Pembrokeshire coast. Rocky outcrops abound in the otherwise flat terrain, the most striking being the miniature peak of Carnllidi over on the left. The fields are small (some of them are very ancient enclosures) and are mainly given over to rough pasture, although occasionally one has been cultivated for early potatoes or vegetables. The original smallholdings are marked by a scattering of cottages, often built where an isolated rock gives shelter from the strong prevailing wind; many of them are now holiday cottages, and a large caravan site on the left is another reminder of an important change in the local economy.

Ignore the next turning on the right, but branch off at the one following, marked by farm buildings. As you turn into this quiet lane, the pinnacled top of the cathedral tower comes into view ahead (the earlier building would have been lower, reputedly to hide it from marauding Norsemen). The lane must be a very old route, lined as it is by traditional earth and stone banks, so it is all the more surprising to pass a well-appointed Edwardian mansion at the point where a sharp bend brings you to the fringes of the city.

Descend into the little valley created by the fast-flowing River Alun and take the right fork at the next junction, passing along a pleasant lane with some fine old houses. All at once the magnificent ruins of the Bishop's Palace are silhouetted ahead as the lane leads right up to the main entrance, an impressive gatehouse. The huge residence was

*St David's Cathedral, reputedly founded by
the patron saint of Wales*

created largely by Bishop Gower in the fourteenth century,
and its arcaded parapet is a famous architectural quirk.

These ruins are well worth a visit, but for the moment
continue past the entrance to a footbridge over the river,
where the west end of the cathedral suddenly looms in front
of you. A short walk up the lane on the other side brings you
to the cathedral entrance.

After your visit, make for the flight of steps opposite the
main door, from the top of which there is a splendid view
over the cathedral and palace to the sea beyond, and pass
through the city's only surviving medieval gate. It brings you
into the city centre – an unassuming road junction – and the
return route starts with a walk down Goat Street (signposted
to Porth Clais). Pass the point where the road to St Justinians
drops away to the right and look out for a new housing
development on the left. Immediately opposite is a large

house called Glanalan, and you turn on to the footpath beside its gate.

This pleasant, tree-lined track reaches an isolated cottage, where a gate gives access to a short drive leading to a road junction. Turn left here and walk the quarter of a mile to a crossroads. Turn right and begin the gentle climb towards a farm built beneath a rock outcrop. You are now out of the valley, and the view behind is of the long, low coastline on the other side of St Bride's Bay, with Skomer Island at its tip. From here, too, you get a final glimpse of the cathedral, backed by its city.

After topping the rise the lane winds down to a junction with the St Justinians road. Turn left and after a quarter of a mile ignore the lane marked Treleddyn Farm but take the lane to the right immediately after. It leads to the cliff top, and a bungalow marks the point where the waymarked Pembrokeshire Coast Path branches to the right.

The path now hugs the cliff top and provides an exhilarating return to Whitesands, with views over some of Britain's finest coastal scenery.

Walk 13
ST GOVAN'S CHAPEL
PEMBROKE
4 miles

St Govan's Chapel has long been an attraction for visitors to south Pembrokeshire. It lies wedged between rocks just above the high-tide mark on a notoriously jagged stretch of coast six miles to the south of Pembroke – a romantic situation that has given rise to many legends, although historical fact about its foundation is harder to come by.

St Govan himself is a mystery. He has been variously identified with King Arthur's knight Gawain, an Irish monk called Gobam, and Cofen, the wife of a sixth-century Celtic chief. The cell which he or she established in this remote place must have gained a widespread reputation because the original building was laboriously replaced in the fifteenth century, and the holy well (now dried up) that stands just below it indicates that it was a place of pilgrimage.

You reach the chapel by a flight of steps from the cliff top. Tradition has it that the number of steps changes each time you go up and down, a fact that is confirmed by the different figures given in each guide book. However, I can state authoritatively that there are 73 steps down and 71 up. The chapel is a simple rectangle containing nothing but a stone altar and a holy water stoup, but the fascinating feature is the cell, roughly carved out of the solid rock at the east end. A notice rightly reminds us that this is consecrated ground, but the fact did not deter nineteenth-century visitors from carving their names on the walls.

Below the chapel a small stone structure marks the site of

the well. The overriding impression here is of the force of the sea. It foams menacingly just below, and has convoluted the cliffs into fantastic shapes, forming remarkable arches and stacks. It must have required extreme hardiness to live in this rugged place.

The walk to the chapel is simple, but it can be extended to make a circular route that takes in a fine stretch of cliff top, a sandy beach and a picturesque series of artificial lakes.

Start by driving to Bosherston, a small village signposted off the B4319 about three and a half miles south of Pembroke. Pass the church and turn left immediately after into a large car park created for visitors to the lakes.

You may now encounter a problem. The direct route to the chapel passes through the Castlemartin artillery range and is closed when firing is in progress. You can check by following the road through the village, past the cafe and pub. The military road branches off here and if a red flag is flying you are out of luck, but you can still enjoy a good walk by following the described route in reverse as far as the cliffs beyond Broad Haven.

In fact the odds are that the road will be open, and on this assumption follow it out of the village and past the official checkpoint. It rises gently to provide a view to the sea ahead and across acres of rough pasture on either side, looking remarkably unscathed. On the sides of the road are stone-faced banks characteristic of Pembrokeshire. It is a short and easy walk to the cliff-top car park and the steps down to the chapel.

On returning to the cliff top climb the stile at the eastern end of the car park and follow the grassy track that begins to move away from the shore (this is still army property and the route is marked by prominent white stakes). The walking is very pleasant on springy cropped turf, and as the path curves round and descends to the cliff edge again there are remarkable views of the rocky coast. Don't let young children run ahead here.

As you continue to follow the white stakes the view to the east is dominated by Stackpole Head, and Caldey Island is

St Govan's Chapel, hidden beneath the Pembrokeshire cliffs

visible in the distance. A stile beside another checkpoint
marks the exit from the range, and the path dips into a hollow
and rises to a gate into a large car park serving the nearby
bathing paradise of Broad Haven. Walk to the top of the car
park, turn right at a wooden hut and then immediately left on
to the waymarked Pembrokeshire Coast Path. It descends by
steps onto the Broad Haven beach. Make for the other side of
the sands where a small stream runs into the sea, then follow
the stream inland for about 300 yards. You will see a footbridge crossing some pretty, miniature 'rapids'. On the other
side ignore the path to the left and continue straight on to
pass round the foot of the Bosherston Pools.

These lakes were created in the nineteenth century as part
of the park landscaping for Stackpole Court, the home of the
Earls of Cawdor. The house is no longer standing, but the
park is owned by the National Trust. The landscaping takes
advantage of natural bluffs and outcrops to produce scenery

rather like the Lake District on a small scale, and the effect is most attractive, especially when the famous water-lilies are flourishing.

The path is now well-defined. It takes you up the east side of the lake, where the scrubby vegetation of the sand dunes is in marked contrast to the thick woodland on the other side of the water. A long, narrow arm of the lakes lies on the right, and you cross it on a short causeway and pass round the foot of wooded bluffs. A second causeway now lies ahead, needing particular care because it is extremely narrow and railed on one side only – passing is difficult and young children will need a firm hand. On the other side a short climb provides a fine general view of the lakes. Descend right to the water's edge for the final stretch of the walk, which ends with another causeway leading back to the car park.

Walk 14
ABERDULAIS FALLS AND CANAL BASIN
NEATH, WEST GLAMORGAN
4 miles

The former industrial areas of South Wales are only just coming into their own as holiday attractions. Of course, there has always been magnificent scenery there, and the legendary valleys have exerted a strong grip on the imaginations of those who know them only through novels and films. Now, a good deal of enterprise is going into developing former industrial sites as tourist attractions.

A good example is Aberdulais, three miles north-east of Neath. The spectacular waterfalls here were long enclosed within the site of an ironworks – the place has been the scene of metal-working for over 200 years, with the fast-flowing water providing power. Now the area is owned by the National Trust, and, in addition to getting a close-up view of the falls themselves (almost frightening after heavy rain) visitors can see an exhibition explaining the history of the site. There is a charge for admission.

Close by is the restored basin at the junction of the old Neath and Tennant canals. Notable features here are an impressive aqueduct and the sunken remains of an ice-breaker, and further developments should make Aberdulais a centre of canal history.

The circular walk that includes these attractions is of great interest, taking in part of a former industrial village, a disused coalmine and a Victorian reservoir.

The starting point is on a lane that branches off the B4434 midway between the centre of Neath and the village of Tonna

ABERDULAIS FALLS AND CANAL BASIN

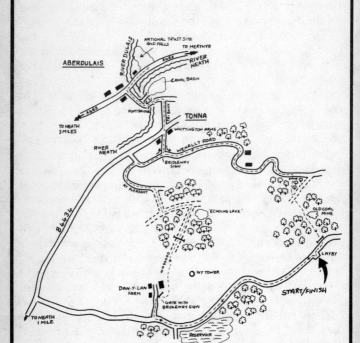

½ MILE

ABERDULAIS

River Dulais

NATIONAL TRUST SITE
AND FALLS

TO MERTHYR

RIVER NEATH

A465

CANAL BASIN

A465

TO NEATH
3 MILES

FOOTBRIDGE

TRAMBANK

TONNA

WHITTINGTON ARMS

WENALLT ROAD

RIVER
NEATH

BRIDLEWAY
SIGN

Mt. PLEASANT

'ECHOING LAKE'

OLD COAL
MINE

B4434

LAYBY

CORACLE

IVY TOWER

START/FINISH

DAN-Y-LAN
FARM

GATE WITH
BRIDLEWAY SIGN

TO NEATH
1 MILE

RESERVOIR

N

- - - -	ROUTE
▬▬▬	ROAD
⊢▬⊣	GATE
▭▭▭	TRACK
〰〰	RIVER

to the north-east. One and a half miles up this lane, park in a layby on the right, just before the top of a long hill.

Begin by walking back down the lane. At this height there are fine views of the Brecon Beacons, behind you, and the lower Neath valley and Swansea Bay ahead. Closer at hand on the right is the Ivy Tower, and eighteenth-century folly built by the wealthy owners of the Gnoll estate.

The lane drops sharply through a double bend, and the open heathland on the left gives way to an ever-deepening wooded ravine bounded by an old stone wall. A section of the wall has been lowered to provide a view of a waterfall pouring into the reservoir which now becomes visible below. It was constructed here in Mosshouse Wood in the early 1890s to supply the houses and industries of Neath, but is now redundant. Just after the iron entrance gates look across the valley to the artificial cascade carrying the water away, a typical piece of fine Victorian engineering.

One hundred yards further on, a wide track on the right bears the sign Dan-y-Lan Farm. Walk along it for a few yards then through the gate on the right (with a public bridleway marker) and diagonally up the slope, passing behind the farm buildings. A well-defined track at the top of the slope leads round to a low broken wall. The path is along the right of this wall, and it soon becomes a wide track taking you down into woodland. At this point there are again good views over Aberdulais and the Neath valley.

After passing through a gate you join another track and turn left, but before going on it is worth making your way through the undergrowth on the right to see the Echoing Lake, a deep pool in an old quarry.

The left turn takes you past a grassed-over spoil heap, and after 50 yards turn right down a stony path that emerges unexpectedly into a respectable suburban road. This is Mount Pleasant in the village of Tonna, and if you follow it down to the bottom it becomes Dolcoed Terrace and then joins Wenallt Road. Turn right here and follow Wenallt Road for 150 yards to the point where a bridleway sign indicates a path down to the left.

The Aberdulais Falls, once used to power machinery

You come out between the Whittington Arms and a church hall near the centre of this old industrial settlement. Continue the descent by crossing the road and taking the lane opposite. This is Tai Bank, and although it is now lined by modern housing the retaining wall hints at the older cottages that must once have stood above the road.

Where Tai Bank joins the main road, signposts point to the restored canal basin. After looking round this, return to the main road, and turn right, pass the Railway Tavern and cross the footbridge over the River Neath. From this bridge there is an excellent view of the shallow-arched aqueduct beyond the railway bridge. Turn right after the footbridge and walk up to the A465 (note the lock at the end of the aqueduct). Go downhill along the main road for about 100 yards and the entrance to the falls is on the left.

After your visit retrace your route across the river, along Tai Bank and up the path beside the Whittington Arms. At the top turn left and follow the lane past a short row of houses on to high moorland. Keep to the lane for a quarter of a mile, ignoring diversions, until it winds round two houses. Shortly after the second house look out for a stile on the right with a public footpath sign.

On crossing the stile you step into thin woodland over a maze of small streams where a coal tramway once ran to the canal at Aberdulais. At the edge of the woodland cross the rough track leading to the road and make for the stile straight ahead up the slope. It marks the start of more woodland, where nature has reclaimed the site of a small coal mine. The relics of industry – cuttings, wharves and broken walls – lie beneath the vegetation, and 100 yards into the wood the bricked-up entrance to the mine, looking like a small railway tunnel, lies just to the left of the path.

As you leave the second belt of trees the path climbs a short stretch of heath to a stile at the top, just to the right of a white house. The layby is 50 yards down the hill.

Walk 15
CARN GOCH HILL FORT
LLANGADOG, DYFED

2 miles

Walks to Iron Age hill forts are always rewarding, partly because of their intrinsic historical interest but also because they usually command the finest views. Unfortunately, many of the best examples involve climbing that can be very demanding for all but the most active. There is one fort, however, that is among the largest in Wales, has rare historical features and can easily be reached on foot.

Carn Goch is situated nine miles south-west of Llandovery, three miles due south of the village of Llangadog.

Although some of the Welsh hill forts have been shown to date from the Bronze Age, most of them were established by a later generation of Celts in the sixth century BC. The word 'fort' can be misleading. Some of the sites are small and obviously designed as hill-top lookout points or places where a community could be gathered for protection as a last resort. Others, however, are so extensive that they could only have been long-term settlements – villages in fact.

Carn Goch is one of the latter. Its compound is vast – covering nearly 30 acres – and only a very large community could have hoped to defend such a circumference. Its defensive features are unusual in that there are none of the customary excavated trenches and ramparts; instead the natural stone ridges are reinforced by thick dry stone walls. The walls were obviously built from stones cleared off the occupied area (immediately below the fort the hill is still covered by loose boulders) and the work involved is further

CARN GOCH HILL FORT

½ MILE

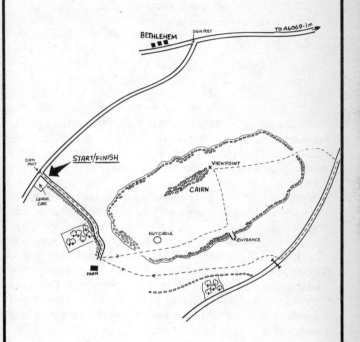

BETHLEHEM

SIGN POST

TO A4069·1m

SIGN POST

START/FINISH

LEAVE CAR

VIEWPOINT

CAIRN

HUT CIRCLE

ENTRANCE

FARM

N

----	ROUTE
===	ROAD
⊢—⊣	GATE
oooo	ROCKS

evidence of the large labour force available and the intention to settle for a long time. Surprisingly, only one hut platform has survived.

Carn Goch has apparently received little attention from archaeologists and not much from officialdom either, so the visitor has the sense of walking directly into remote history, as though the place had remained untouched since the occupants departed.

To reach the start of the walk take the A4069 (Swansea) road out of Llangadog and after two and a quarter miles turn right onto a minor road signposted to Bethlehem (a hamlet named after its chapel). Just before you enter the hamlet, the fort is signposted down a lane to the left. Follow the lane for about three quarters of a mile until you see another signpost pointing to a farm track on the left. You will please the local farmer if you park here rather than cluttering up his lane further on.

The walk up the lane is easy and attractive anyway. On the left rough, bracken-covered pasture leads up to the eastern defences of Carn Goch, while to the right the low-lying fields show signs of centuries of farming activity, with the earth and stone banks that were the earliest form of enclosure. Note, too, the wall that lines the lane. It is built with the awkward, lumpy stone of the area, but at some time an attempt was made to train a hedge along the top. As a result several substantial trees have straight horizontal branches at wall-top level.

Opposite the farm entrance a signpost directs you up the hill on a rough grass track, and after 300 yards you enter the fort through a break in the defensive wall, which at this point is now an immense heap of stones. Walk straight ahead and after about 50 yards look out for the hut circle to the left of the path. If you now follow a route just inside the defence works on the right you will see an entrance way that has been lined with vertical slabs. (It is likely that the whole inner wall was lined with these slabs originally).

To discover the reason for the camp's position you should now cross the enclosure to one end of the impressive summit

Sheep now graze on the ramparts of Carn Goch hill fort

cairn and look north. The remarkable view takes in many miles of the Tywi valley, and the river itself can be overlooked for a long way east and west, meandering noticeably just opposite the viewpoint. A glance at a map of the area will show what an important strategic route the valley was in this region of complex hills.

From the cairn follow one of the tracks that lead to the eastern end of the enclosure and walk down the short stretch of hillside – with its coarse vegetation and covering of stones it may well not have changed much since the Iron Age. By contrast, the hills in front of you have been reclaimed from waste right to the top to produce healthy-looking pasture.

Join the metalled lane below and turn right. In front of the gate barring the road take the grass track on the right that soon begins to run beside a dry-stone wall. As you wind your way between boulders you get a vivid impression of the task that faced the very early farmers who had to clear and improve the land. After passing a copse of very old trees the path runs below one of the most impressive stretches of rampart to give an enemy's-eye view of the fort, and it must be remembered that the original defensive walls must have been higher and steeper than they are now. Part of this length has been built on top of a natural cliff.

The track now moves away from the wall to lead you back to the farm entrance.

Walk 16
PARTRISHOW CHURCH
ABERGAVENNY, GWENT
3½ miles

If Wales lacks the wealth of splendid parish churches that
attract so many visitors in England, there is compensation in
the number of small and remote churches that have retained
their primitive atmosphere of rough-hewn sturdiness.
Throughout Wales there are concealed churches that were so
difficult to get to that they escaped the attentions of both the
Puritan reformers of the seventeenth century and the well-
meaning Victorian restorers. Consequently they still have
features that disappeared from most English churches a long
time ago.

Partrishow church near Abergavenny must be one of the
best examples. Tucked away in the hills, far from any
present-day settlement, it is still not easy to find. Reaching it
by car involves a long uphill drive on a narrow, nerve-racking
lane, and the walker has a far pleasanter approach.

Officially, this is the church of Merthyr Issui at Patricio.
Tradition has it that the church was founded by a Celtic
missionary named Issui who had a cell in the dingle below the
present building. He was murdered by a traveller he had
taken in, and his cell became a place of pilgrimage, with a
holy well nearby. A wealthy man who was cured of leprosy at
the well gave the money to establish a church, and there is
historical evidence of its consecration here in the eleventh
century.

The earliest parts of the building are late Norman, and it is
likely that the unstable ground led to rebuilding at an early

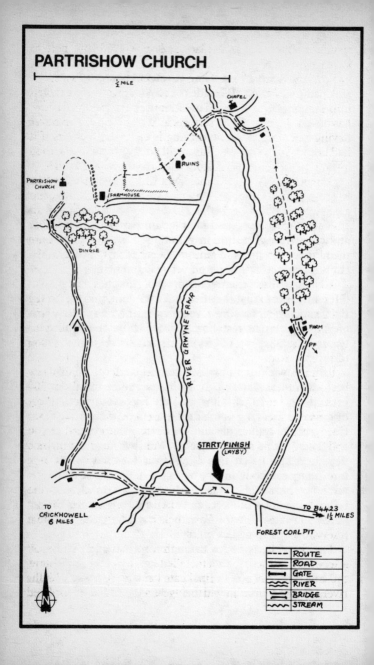

PARTRISHOW CHURCH

½ MILE

CHAPEL

RUINS

PARTRISHOW
CHURCH

FARMHOUSE

DINGLE

RIVER GRWYNE FAWR

FARM

PF

START/FINISH
(LAYBY)

TO
CRICKHOWELL
6 MILES

TO B4423
1½ MILES

FOREST COAL PIT

N

- - - -	ROUTE
▬▬▬	ROAD
▬█▬	GATE
≈≈≈	RIVER
▤▤	BRIDGE
～～～	STREAM

stage. Similar work took place as late as 1908, but here at Partrishow there is the chance to see a church interior that has remained largely unchanged since the middle ages.

A pamphlet available inside the church gives very detailed information, but it is worth mentioning here that Partrishow has one of the finest rood screens in Wales, unusual in never having been painted. The carving is crisp and looks as if it had been done yesterday. Rarer still is the survival of the rood loft above it, reached by stone steps in an adjacent wall.

Other unusual features include a tiny chapel or cell at the west end with a squint hole giving a view into the church, and a massive font dating from well before the Norman conquest. The walls bear traces of medieval painting, with a very clear and dramatic representation of Time as a skeleton. There are many more examples of unusual work, and they make the church a very worthwhile objective for a walk.

To reach the starting point leave Abergavenny on the A465 (Hereford) road, and after five miles turn left onto the B4423 at Llanfihangel Crucorney. After one and a half miles a lane on the left is signposted Forest Coal Pit. Go up this lane for two miles and park in a layby with a phone box at the junction of several roads.

Begin by walking up the rough lane that leads uphill a few yards from the phone box. It climbs steeply for about 300 yards then levels off after passing two cottages. A short distance further on a sign indicates a public footpath to Cwm Coedycerrig; ignore this and the narrow track ahead of you and follow the main lane round to the left. After passing some farm buildings it becomes a grassy path with a gate opening into pleasant woodland.

The path now descends steadily with a steep drop to the valley bottom on the left, and the loudest sound is that of the fast-flowing Grwyne Fawr below, rushing down from a reservoir high up in the hills.

The descent continues through a second gate, and soon afterwards the path joins a metalled lane by a cottage. Follow the lane downhill until a final gate brings you into an idyllic riverside spot with an old bridge and a curiously isolated

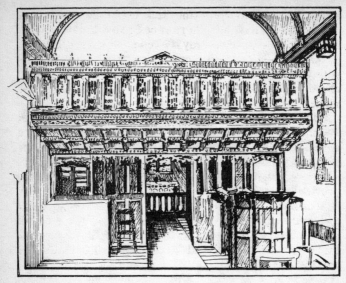

The magnificent rood screen and loft at Partrishow church

chapel. It is not the usual late-Victorian structure; it bears the
date 1837 and is long and low, with simple accommodation at
one end.

Cross the bridge and walk the few yards up to a minor
road. Immediately opposite is a modern stile with the official
look of a waymarked path. It gives access to a stony lane that
shortly passes some ruined buildings.

When you have passed through the first gate the path
disappears and you need to look carefully for the next stile. It
is 100 yards away up the slope on the other side of the field in
a direction roughly half-right from the gate. The small yellow
arrows now become reassuring because the path passes
through farm buildings very close to an old farmhouse.
Stone-built and leaning, it must date at least from the seventeenth century if not earlier, and its garden has some superb
topiary work.

The way is now through a gate close to the house, up the

farm drive and round to the back of the house through another gate. Here the path runs beside a fine garden wall, and there is a chance to study the venerable stone tiles of the farmhouse roof. You soon emerge on to open hillside; the path curves to the left and Partrishow church lies directly ahead, hugging the hillside and well-hidden even at close range.

After your visit leave by way of the lych gate and walk down the lane that drops quickly to reach a bridge over a stream. This is a very picturesque place with a view from the bridge down a steep wooded dingle – the original dwelling place of St Issui. The lane now rises steadily and levels off to provide another panorama of remote hills and valleys.

Soon after the final descent begins there is an unsignposted fork in the lane. Go to the left, wind your way down the hill and turn left again at the next junction. You cross a river bridge, pass another very old farmhouse over on the right and emerge at the layby.

Walk 17
CASTELL COCH
CARDIFF, SOUTH GLAMORGAN
4 miles

Castell Coch is the castle to visit when you are tired of visiting castles. It stands on the northern fringes of Cardiff close to the A470 at Tongwynlais, and is not to be confused with Cardiff Castle, which is much closer to the city centre. The two have much in common, however, since both belonged to the Bute family, the great Cardiff property magnates, and both received attention from the third Marquess and his talented architect William Burges.

In 1865 Lord Bute commissioned Burges to restore the thirteenth-century Cardiff Castle; in fact, it was virtually rebuilt in an extravagantly romantic medieval style (it is open to the public and well worth visiting). In 1871 Burges was asked to deal similarly with the smaller castle to the north, perched on a commanding hill and in an area earmarked by the Marquess for vineyards. The result was a completely un-British castle featuring solid round towers and stubby spires, a style more in keeping with the Rhineland.

With its fake medieval features, including drawbridge, portcullis and dungeon, it has been likened to something out of Disneyland, but its real glory is its exotic interior, the result of superb artistry and craftsmanship. Particularly fine are the banqueting hall, the drawing room (with amusing murals based on Aesop's fables) and a bedroom designed for Lady Bute, featuring a castellated washstand and other unusual luxuries. The total effect is a fantasy in uninhibited patterns and colours that contrast strangely with their solid setting.

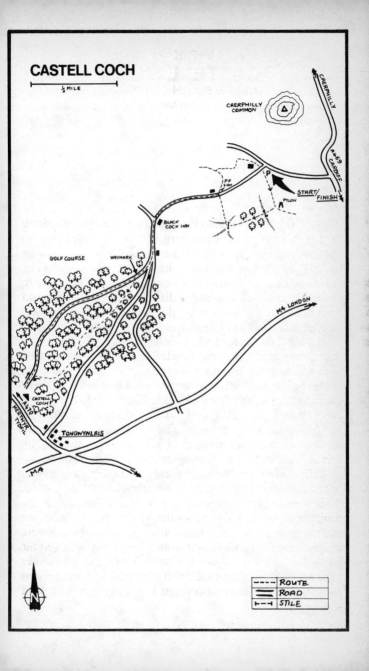

CASTELL COCH

½ MILE

CAERPHILLY COMMON

CAERPHILLY

A469 CARDIFF

P.F. SIGN

P

START / FINISH

PYLON

BLACK COCK INN

GOLF COURSE

WAYMARK

M4 LONDON

CASTELL COCH

A470 MERTHYR TYDIL

TONGWYNLAIS

M4

N

---- ROUTE
=== ROAD
⊢—⊣ STILE

The castle is now in the care of Cadw, the Welsh Historic Monuments Commission, and one of the rooms has an interesting exhibition explaining the restoration and other work carried out by Burges.

Considering that Castell Coch is surrounded by Cardiff, Caerphilly and the industrial valley of the Taff, the walk to it is remarkably rural. The starting point is on the southern edge of Caerphilly Common. About one and a quarter miles south of Caerphilly Castle on the A469 to Cardiff you pass a prominent domed hill on the right. Take the next right turn after this and then turn left at the first junction. Turn left again immediately onto a track where the car can be left.

This track is in fact the start of the walk. It drops to the bottom of a shallow valley and then becomes a path leading up the bracken-covered hill opposite. The top of the hill brings an unexpected panorama of the sea, or rather the Bristol channel, with the Somerset coast on the horizon. The tower blocks of Cardiff stand out below. At this point, close to an electricity pylon, the main path curves to the left; ignore it and make for the stile in the adjacent fence.

On the other side there is a pleasant stretch of walking on a broad ridge and through a sparse copse. The path is not completely clear, but keep to the top of the ridge and follow its further slope down to a second stile in the fence that comes in from the right. After crossing it bear half right and walk down the large sloping field towards a cottage visible at the bottom. Opposite the cottage a stile of tubular steel gives access to a minor road. Turn left here.

A short distance along the road the Black Cock Inn stands at a road junction. Continue round to the left past the post box and pass the entrance to the new Castell Heights Golf Club, where there is a view of the bare dome of Craig-yr-Allt. The road now descends to a fork at a group of white houses. Take the lane to the right, and at the bottom of the short hill branch right again onto a forestry road signposted Tair Onen. After 50 yards a waymark directs you off to the left, and this very pleasant path passes through the southern edge of the forest to rejoin the main track, which you take to the

Castell Coch, like a Disneyland castle

left. Within a few yards a gate marks the entrance to the castle grounds. You reach the castle by way of a steep descent through mature beech trees.

Start the walk back by returning to the gate. There are several paths through the forest, but waymarking in this direction is practically non-existent, and the safest (and shortest) route is the wide main track which cuts straight through on the northern side. On reaching the forest entrance retrace the route past the Black Cock and pass the stile you previously crossed.

When you reach a scattering of houses the lane begins a sudden rise, and at the foot of the hill a signposted footpath leads off to the left. Follow this and bear right at the junction of paths halfway to the top. If you look west at this point the view could be of rural mid-Wales rather than the industrial-ised south, but the illusion is quickly shattered when you reach the top and find the sprawl of Caerphilly spread out below (the famous castle is just out of sight in the valley).

Two paths cross here, and if you wish to extend the walk you can explore Caerphilly Common by continuing straight ahead down the hill or by taking the path to the left. Otherwise turn right and return past the back of a farmhouse to the road junction.

Walk 18
WINTOUR'S LEAP
CHEPSTOW, GWENT
4 miles

In 1642 a local Royalist commander, Sir John Wintour, escaped from pursuing Roundheads near Chepstow by urging his horse over a cliff and swimming the River Wye beneath. Ever since then the spot where he launched himself off has been known as Wintour's Leap.

It has to be said that this is an unlikely story, not least because the cliff in question is about 200 feet high and sheer, with very hard ground below it, and local historians reckon that the actual site has become confused. Nevertheless the Leap is a magnificent viewpoint on a river that is noted for romantic scenery and dramatic geography.

In the late eighteenth and early nineteenth centuries a trip down the Wye was one of Britain's most popular tourist journeys, and no doubt Wintour's Leap was an eagerly-awaited landmark, along with Symonds Yat and the Wyndcliff. These last two famous viewpoints have been made very accessible with car parks and paths, but the Leap presents a problem since it consists of a narrow strip of ground between the cliff edge and a busy road. Motorists expecting to be able to stop are frustrated, but the walker can enjoy superb views over Longhope Reach to Chepstow and South Wales beyond. To the west is the Lancaut Peninsula, where the Wye goes through one of its tortuous meanders, and the view in this direction is dominated by the wooded Piercefield Cliffs on the other side of the river.

Nowadays, Wintour's Leap is almost in the Chepstow

WINTOUR'S LEAP

½ MILE

LANCAUT CHURCH

WINTOUR'S LEAP

WOODCROFT

CLIFFS

ARCHWAY

PEN MOEL

TUTSHILL

RIVER WYE

HALL

TOWER

PUB

A48
GLOUCESTER

IRON ROAD BRIDGE

BRUNEL'S RAILWAY BRIDGE

START/FINISH

CHEPSTOW CASTLE

---	ROUTE
===	ROAD
⊢-⊣	GATE
⊢=⊣	STILE
⧦	BRIDGE

N

suburbs, but it is possible to reach it by way of a tranquil walk through landscape that is unique to the Wye Valley.

The car can be left in the car park by the entrance to Chepstow next to the Castle, the town's leading attraction and well worth visiting. Begin the walk down the road to the river and cross by the narrow iron road bridge. From here you can appreciate the maritime atmosphere of the Wye at Chepstow.

On the other side of the bridge is a pedestrian lane straight ahead. Walk up it, cross the A48 at the top and take the minor road immediately opposite. After about 150 yards look for a stile on the left just before the first house (This section of the route is part of the Offa's Dyke long-distance path and has the distinctive white acorn waymark.)

Cross the stile and follow the path up the rising field, passing on the right the remains of an old stone tower, possibly a watch-tower or beacon of the sixteenth century. You now walk towards the belt of trees in the corner of the field, cross a stile and proceed in the shadow of a long stone wall. In the corner created by a section of wall jutting out at a right angle there is another stile giving access to a short passage from which you emerge into the private drive of the nearby house. The owners have generously allowed the path to pass virtually through their back garden.

A few yards down the drive cross the stile on the left and start to traverse a fine piece of parkland, dominated by a rather exotic Edwardian villa on the far side. This is Pen Moel, and you enter its wooded estate on a narrow path bounded by a high wall and an impressive rock outcrop. There now starts a most peaceful descent through trees that provide occasional glimpses of high, sheer cliffs on your right, the ones from which Wintour was supposed to have made his leap. As the path winds along it passes the remains of old quarries, and at weekends you will also come across rock-climbers.

The path is descending all the time towards the river, which is wide, brown, silent and slightly sinister, and when you finally reach the bank you are at the point where a sharp

Chepstow castle, starting point for the walk to Wintour's Leap

bend marks the start of the giant meander round the Lancaut Peninsula. Having touched the bank the path now re-ascends a little to run through a fringe of trees with occasional open stretches, and on the peak of the bend it is possible to see, when the tide is low, the relics of riverside installations connected with the quarries.

When you reach a novel stile made by the army out of tubular steel, look for a path on the right leading up to the ruins of St James's Church, Lancaut, last used in the mid-nineteenth century.

On the other side of the church a clear track begins to climb back into the woodland. It eventually joins a level path, and you turn right close to a pair of old limekilns. After 400 yards the path meets a minor road which in turn leads to the B4228. Turn right again, and at the sharp bend a short way down you can stand on Wintour's Leap itself.

A little way down the road a sign tells you that you are entering Woodcroft, and 100 yards further on a stile marks the start of a path along the top of the cliffs (young children will need a firm hand here). Only the first short stretch is at all dangerous – the path gradually moves away from the clifftop, passing the backs of houses and giving a final vertiginous view of a huge quarry. When you reach the top of a cul-de-sac with a house on the right, continue straight ahead until you finally emerge through an old archway into the village of Tutshill.

The route is now beside the B4228 until you reach the village centre. Look for the Memorial Hall on the right and take the road that branches off next to it, signposted to Mopla. A short downhill walk will bring you back to the top of the pedestrian lane leading down to the bridge and thence to the castle car park.